12 Lessons On Sushi

Become an Expert on Ordering,
Eating, and Making the Best Sushi

A Guide by
27Press

www.27press.com

12 Lessons On Sushi: Become an Expert on Ordering, Eating, and Making the Best Sushi

Published by 27Press
www.27press.com

First Edition

November, 2013

ISBN-10: 0-9887705-3-9
ISBN-13: 978-0-9887705-3-9

v.0103

Disclaimer

Although the author, editors, and publisher have made every effort to ensure that the information in this book was correct at press time, the author, editors, and publisher do not assume and hereby disclaim any liability to any party for any loss, damage, or disruption caused by errors or omissions, whether such errors or omissions result from negligence, accident, or any other cause. This book is not intended as a substitute for the medical advice of physicians. The reader should regularly consult a physician in matters relating to his/her health and particularly with respect to any symptoms that may require diagnosis or medical attention.

Thank You

I want to extend a special thank you to everyone who helped with this book. Many people provided ideas, comments, edits, and suggestions along the way toward the completion of this project. A few of those people are listed here in alphabetical order:

Ashley Jarvis Barrett
Kobe Kobayashi
Margaret Jarvis
Patrick Tinsley
Sarah Caragianis
Takeshi Trinitapoli
Wayne Conwell
Yoshitaka (Fred) Yamada

Thank you for all your help,
David J. Kosmider
Founder, 27Press

27Press

We produce excellent guides
like this one on a variety of
different topics.

10% of all author royalties are donated to
awesome non-profit organizations.

Details available on our website.

www.27Press.com

Questions or comments?

Email us:
news@27press.com

12 Lessons
On Sushi

Contents

Introduction

I'm not making art, I'm making sushi.
-Masaharu Morimoto, Japanese Chef

Welcome to the world of sushi! This book will provide you with comprehensive knowledge on the topics of ordering, eating, making, and enjoying a variety of different traditional and modern types of sushi. Even if you have been eating sushi for years, you will likely pick up several new bits of knowledge along the way to help you enjoy sushi even more. While this book contains some information about Japanese culture, it's written primarily for American and European readers and focuses on what they might typically encounter in their local sushi restaurant.

Whether you are eating at your local sushi bar

or you happen find yourself in a traditional Tokyo sushi-ya, the knowledge in this book will allow you to confidently enjoy the best sushi the world has to offer (and maybe even help you impress your friends and colleagues with your newfound knowledge of sushi along the way). Remember, this book is only the first part of a multi-step learning process. Only experiencing sushi for yourself will allow you to truly understand it. Starting out, you should try as many styles and types of sushi as you can get your hands on to find out what you like the most. Please also check out our online resources at the link below, it includes more links to additional information about sushi, including recommended additional reading, videos, and images, anything that is not easy to include in this book format.

Japanese Language

Japanese is written in characters, or logographs, which represent a word or meaning. One of the Japanese systems of writing is called Romaji, it is essentially a translation of Japanese words into Latin characters. In this book we have provided the Romaji spelling of many of the words associated with sushi so that Western readers can become familiar with them. The word *sushi* itself is the

Romaji form of 寿司. For additional help with pronunciation of these terms, our online resources guide provides a list of important sushi-related terms along with links to native Japanese speakers saying each word.

The online resources are available here:
27Press.com/sushi

Lesson 1
What is Sushi?

There's a lot of prep work in the rice. Making the rice is actually the most labor-intensive part of making sushi, but it's a very important step.
-Alice Yip

Any dish that includes the specially prepared sushi rice (*su-meshi*) is a type of sushi. It is the rice itself that makes something "sushi," not fish, as as is commonly believed in Western countries.

Sashimi, which is a dish of several pieces of sliced, raw fish, is commonly served before or with sushi, but is not "sushi" because it does not include any rice, more information about sashimi will be covered in Lesson 7.

In *The Story of Sushi*, Trevor Corson writes, "Japan's native religion, Shinto, starts with the belief that everything—trees, foxes, fish, and samurai swords—possess it's own spirit... Rice seems especially sacred because it is Japan's staple food."

Rice is the second largest grain crop worldwide, behind wheat, and makes up a large part of the Japanese diet; approximately 30% of total food consumed. Though rice is a source of some protein, it's not a complete protein, and it is generally served with other proteins such as fish and meat.

Types of Rice

There are more than 40,000 varieties of rice grown throughout the world. Rice is categorized into long, medium, and short grains. Each has a different absorption rate and the cooking water is adjusted accordingly. Long grain rice tends to be fluffier and more fragrant and hold its shape better after cooking. Medium grain rice absorbs flavors well and becomes more sticky when cooked. It is used in dishes such as risotto and paella. Short grain rice, or Japanese rice, has a sweet aroma and firm sticky grains that hold flavors well. The stickiness also makes it a little easier to eat with chopsticks and holds ingredients better in dishes like sushi. Its sweet nutty flavor is excellent for sushi and puddings, and great all by itself as a side dish. Japanese rice is also used for sake production. Westerners frequently refer to Japanese rice as sushi rice.

Preparation

Great care is taken in sushi restaurants to make the perfect rice. Sushi rice has only a few ingredients; short-grain rice, water, sugar, salt, konbu (Japanese kelp), and rice vinegar. The sushi rice is cooked and then left to steam for about 15 minutes. The vinegar, with the sugar, salt, and konbu is then drizzled over the rice (in a non-metalic bowl, preferably wooden) and gently but thoroughly mixed with a wodden paddle, so as not to smash the grains but to coat the rice well.

While the basic recipe may seem simple, sushi chef apprentices spend years learning how to make the rice correctly. Typically, an apprentice spends about five years training with a master sushi chef before he is allowed to prepare the rice. Following very strict instructions, he will work diligently to refine his sushi rice until the master chef is satisfied. The preparation technique for each individual sushi-ya is a much coveted and prized secret. What really sets sushi restaurants apart, and is the backbone of any great sushi restaurant, is the caliber of its sushi rice. And simply put, great sushi rice is the result of years of hard work and formal training.

Sushi History: "Sushi" has included many different types of food over the last 2,000 years, but most of what we know as sushi today was developed in Japan during the Edo period (1603 to 1868). Japan was a busy place, and was in need of a way to be able to buy and consume food in a quick and dependable fashion. Hayazushi, meaning "fast sushi," was developed as a street food, a food that could be bought at a portable stand and consumed with fingers or chopsticks in a quick way.

Lesson 2
Seafood Industry

I either buy my first choice, or I buy nothing.
If ten tuna are for sale, only one can be the
best. I buy that one.
-Hiroki Fujita, Tokyo Fish Market Buyer

While technically "sushi" is any food that includes the special sushi rice, good quality rice is relatively easy to get to the sushi shop year round. The sushi industry really revolves around seafood, especially tuna. In *The Sushi Economy*, Sasha Issenberg writes that "Until the Meiji era, the highest-quality sushi shops preferred blue marlin, and tuna was—along with oily mackerel, saury, gizzard shad, and sardines—seen as a lower-grade fish."

Tastes have changed a lot in the last hundred years.

The explosion of sushi restaurants around the world since the 1970's has only been possible due to the technologies that have been developed to quickly move fresh fish, by air to markets far from where they are harvested. Whether directly or indirectly, the seafood industry provides hundreds of millions of jobs worldwide.

Bluefin Tuna

It is the last week of June, and Bluefin tuna are migrating toward the Northern Atlantic waters. This is the time of year when many US based fishing vessels set out in search of these fish. Long hours before the sun begins to rise above the eastern horizon a large fishing boat sets sail from a harbor in Gloucester, Maine. The captain and crew are getting ready to track and catch tuna, specifically the large, Bluefin tuna, often called Black Diamonds for their value. Setting out in darkness is essential because these migratory fish travel far out in the ocean, where the water is deep and the currents are bitingly cold. The boats have a long way to travel to catch the larger fish that they are after. Everyone has a job to do on this fishing boat and each crew member is busy with their own list of duties.

One of the crew members has even been instructed by Tsukiji "tuna technicians" exactly what features to look for when the tuna are being captured and brought on-board the ship. The finest fish with the best shape and form will bring the most money at auction. As the sun first makes its appearance the dark nighttime sky gives way to pale shades of peach, blue and warm yellows. Although the thought of a successful fishing trip is top on everyone's minds it is impossible to ignore the beauty of this ocean scene. The boat continues to travel farther away from the Maine shoreline, pushing its way into the deeper waters as the captain monitors an elaborate display of GPS screens, radars, and fish-finding equipment.

The captain and crew know that these fish are rapidly adding layers of fat to protect them from the colder waters. The electronic monitors on the boat are searching the waters in order to help pinpoint exactly where the fish are located. The crew and captain are well aware that this is the time of year when larger tuna are more readily caught and they are now anxious to find them. Spotter planes have also been employed to help the boat locate schools of Bluefin. The pilot will receive a portion of the fishing profits.

The boat anchors in a prime fishing site and heavy poles and tackle are used to catch the tuna. The crew and captain are pleased with the size and length of many of these fish. There are several tuna that are almost 6 feet long and weigh more than 400 pounds. As each fish is being brought on-board it is killed with an electric harpoon. These large tuna must be killed swiftly to prevent stress from tainting the meat with unpleasant flavors. Other crew members begin gutting the fish as quickly as possible. The tuna are immediately frozen at a low temperature of -76°F (-60°C). The fish are packaged into containers and placed on ice.

There are some buyers from Japan who are waiting for the fishing boat to arrive back in the Gloucester harbor. The tuna are inspected and graded by these buyers. After checking to ascertain the current prices in the Tuskiji fresh fish market the tuna will be purchased, repacked in more ice and then loaded into large trucks. The trucks take the fish to JFK Airport in New York. It is now time for the ice-packed tuna to be loaded onto cargo airplanes. The planes will take the fish to Japan. The tuna arrive in Tokyo 15 hours later.

The Tuskiji Fish Market Auction in Tokyo

begins at 5:30 AM. The auction lasts for about half an hour. During this short period of time each of the fish is cut so that the bidders can closely look at the texture, fatty content, and coloring. In *Tuna: A Love Story*, by Richard Ellis writes, "Years of experience enable the buyers at Tsukiji to examine the fish with an eye (and nose) toward identifying the richest reddest meat with the highest fat content."

Those tuna with higher amounts of fat and marbled flesh command the highest bids. Hand gestures are the signals used by bidders at Tuskiji and the action is fast and furious. The auctioneer calls out information and bids almost too fast for onlookers to understand. Six separate fish are sold to six individual bidders in a single minutes. Today there will be more than 2,000 freshly frozen tuna available and each one sells quickly to the highest bidder. The Bluefin tuna that were caught near Gloucester, Maine are among the first to be sold.

Sustainability

The issue of sustainability is a very real concern. The oceans house over a million species of plants and animals and cover over two-thirds of the planet. The ocean food chain has supported mankind for thousands of years, but it is currently becoming overtaxed. Pollution, climate changes, poorly regulated fishing practices, and increased demand have all taken their toll on the oceans' biological limits. The good news is that there is a concerted effort among environmental groups, governments (especially those whose people depend heavily on the marine ecosystem), and the private sector, devoted to protecting the seafood supply into the future. Marine protected areas are being established to nurture species identified as endangered, and policies have been developed to achieve a more sustainable worldwide fishery management system.

There's a huge effort on the part of the Japanese government to ensure the reefs are kept clean and stocked with fish. In addition to the naturally occurring reefs, the government spends millions and sometimes billions annually to construct artificial reefs to make sure there's always a farmable supply of fish. The government also provides subsidies to industries and businesses that wish to construct reefs, with the stipulation that the government oversees construction and implementation.

As more wild fish populations become unsustainable, and others fishermen to use more fuel to bring in the same size and quantity of fish, farm raised fish have steadily grown in popularity over the last couple decades. Worldwide levels of farm raised fish production have overtaken that of beef production. Fish farming facilities run the gamut from small ponds to huge high tech facilities that use all manner of methods to breed, hatch, and raise over 100 species of fish. The farm raised fish industory is not without its detractors; it takes many, many little fish to feed the larger fish that people consume, prompting the claim that the practice is not sound. Some believe farmed fish are also less healthy and lower quality than wild fish.

Casson Trenor is a leading advocate for the sustainability movement as it relates to the sushi industry. His book, *Sustainable Sushi*, provides a thorough account of what sustainability means for the industry, how sushi consumers can alter their eating habits to help this cause, and detailed information about each individual sea creature one might encounter in a sushi bar and how that animal is harvested.

Sushi History: Currently tuna, especially bluefin, is in high demand, but that has not always the case. Today's much prized bluefin toro (the fatty fish underbelly) was considered by the Japanese to be almost inedible and was usually destined for the poor working class (or sometimes even cat food). In fact, tuna was so hated that street vendors wouldn't even touch it and it was commonly referred to with disgust as gezakana (inferior fish). The Japanese diet began to imitate the Western diet following World War II, and they began to consume more fatty meats and fish. Also, with refrigeration came wider distribution, and tuna spread to the West and gained popularity. So popular, that today, certain species of tuna are in danger of becoming extinct. Recently, Northern bluefin tuna was nominated to be included in the "complete international trade ban" category at the Convention on International Trade in Endangered Species. Because menu listings can sometimes be inaccurate or indifferent, it can be difficult to determine exactly what species of tuna you may be eating. Some conservation minded consumers have opted to avoid tuna entirely and substitute other equally delicious seafood instead.

Lesson 3
Nigiri

You've got loggers and fishermen in Seattle who didn't know what sushi was a decade ago, eating it at the ballpark and wearing headbands with kanji on them. That's quite a transformation.
-Robert Whiting, Journalist

Nigirizushi, or "hand-formed sushi," is the sushi preparation consisting of a small ball of sushi rice under a proportional piece of thinly sliced raw seafood or other topping, and is one of the most common and recognizable sushi presentations. In his book *The Connoisseur's Guide to Sushi*, Dave

Lowry writes "The rewards of finger foods explain, in part at least, the popularity of sandwiches, beer nuts, and week-old lime Jell-O cubes, and it's one reason why nigiri sushi is what most people think of when they hear 'sushi.'"

The topping, called neta, is usually a piece of fish such as salmon or tuna, but also can be other seafood like shrimp and octopus, cooked freshwater eel, or even egg. The sushi chef commonly adds a touch of wasabi between the rice and the fish, giving the dish ample flavor without any sauces or seasoning. However if you do choose to dip your nigiri sushi in a sauce, remember to dip only the fish side; dipping the rice side could cause your nigiri to fall apart too quickly.

An order of nigiri almost always includes two pieces. It is very rare to find a place that does not follow this tradition. Nigiri was a street food sold from carts originally, and is meant to be eaten with your hands. Just pick it up and put it in your mouth. Of course, if you don't feel comfortable doing that, using your chopsticks is fine as well, but try to eat the whole piece in one bite. It may seem awkwardly large and take some getting used to, but if you try to bite it in half, it will most likely fall apart.

There is a variation of nigiri, called Temari.

Typical nigiri is an oblong shape of rice with a strip of fish on the top, temari is a ball of rice and a square piece of fish, sometimes decorated on the top with strips of scallions or other things, then tightly compacted into a sphere.

Below are some common ingredients, or *neta* that you will encounter on nirigi. Many of these are used as sashimi as well as in the other types of sushi, especially *maki*, as described in the next lesson. This is certainly not a complete list, but the ones that you will probably encounter most often, and if you are new to sushi and sashimi, some of these are the ones you will want to try first.

Tuna (Akami)

When people picture sushi, it is most likely some cut of tuna that they are thinking of because the fish has become an iconic choice. Akami is a cut of tuna that does not have much fat and is deep red in color. Blue fin tuna has been commonly used, but true bluefin has been getting more and more expensive in recent years and other types are commonly used now. Its taste can be described as uncomplicated yet potent.

Fatty Tuna (Toro)

The flesh that comes from the belly of a tuna fish is known as fatty tuna. It is a cut of flesh that is primarily used in sushi to showcase its texture. There is only a small amount of fatty tuna available to harvest per fish and so it is found in the most expensive sushi. It is creamy in taste and extremely oily, so it melts on the tongue. It is sometimes served lightly grilled, to emphasize its smooth properties.

Salmon (Sake)

Salmon has only been incorporated in sushi in recent times. It is a less traditional ingredient but has become extremely popular. The oily bright orange flesh is mild in flavor and is typically served in a citrus-based, salty dish along with wasabi. It is often served both raw and cooked (usually smoked).

Egg Omelette (Tomago)

Tomago is a type of sushi based around an egg omelette. The dish is sweet and is sometimes eaten at the end of a meal, similar to a dessert, or sometimes eaten at the beginning as a test of the chef's skills. Sushi chefs cook the egg in different ways and adapt it to show off their skills. This is a way for sushi chefs to show their ingenuity and creativity. Tomago should be prepared over a charcoal flame for a fluffy omelette.

Mackerel (Saba)

Saba is on typically the more affordable end of the range of sushi available. Mackerel is quick to go bad and so it is typically cured to prevent this, rather than being served raw. Mackerel is served after it has been cured in salt for approximately two hours, then rinsed in rice vinegar. It has a somewhat dry taste and is accompanied by wasabi. Raw mackerel is a local delicacy in areas where fisherman will bring the live fish to a restaurant so it can be prepared and eaten immediately.

Yellowtail (Hamachi)

Hamachi is a luxury fish. Yellowtail are known by different names according to their size and age—this is to distinguish their different flavors at these stages. Hamachi refers to yellowtail fish that are a year old and approximately one foot in size. Wild yellowtail yields an oily flesh with a sweet citrus flavor that is quite bold, making flavor pairings difficult.

Cooked Shrimp (Ebi)

Ebi refers to the cooked shrimp used in many kinds of sushi. Expensive shrimp is sweeter and juicier, similar to lobster meat. More affordable shrimp can be equally delicious, just smaller and slightly lighter in flavor. The shrimp is typically cooked by boiling, but can also be steamed. Steaming is the preferable method as this way no natural sweetness is lost. Raw shrimp is also sometimes served, and referred to as Amaebi.

Octopus (Tako)

Tako refers to the octopus meat used in sushi and sashimi. It is always the leg that is used and for sushi it is poached, the tough meat is thinly sliced. Octopus flesh smells sweet but it is actually quite mild in flavor and this is why cooking it is preferable. Tako is specially prepared before cooking to avoid a rubbery texture—it is washed in salt and tenderized with a peeled radish to impart flavor.

Squid (Ika)

Squid is not often seen in sushi as the tough flesh can prove difficult to prepare. The hood is served raw while the tentacles are boiled. Ika is chewy and sweet flavors develop as you eat it. It has a creamy texture and can be accompanied by ginger to contrast its natural properties. Squid is translucent when fresh, quickly turning opaque. Like octopus, squid is also enjoyed as sashimi, where it is thinly sliced and served with noodles and broth.

Freshwater Eel (Unagi)

Unagi refers to eels that are caught or farmed in freshwater. Freshwater eel is never eaten raw—the flesh would be unpleasant; too oily and tough. Cooking eel is a special skill even for a sushi chef. Unagi is most often cooked over an open flame then steamed. This process rids the flesh of excess fat and then makes it soft and fluffy. It is grilled again while being coated in a sauce made of the eel trimmings, sugar, rice wine and soy sauce. Freshwater eel is sweeter than its saltwater counterpart.

Saltwater Eel (Anago)

Saltwater eels are one of the oldest traditional ingredients in sushi because saltwater eels were at one time plentiful in Tokyo Bay and so their popularity has endured. It is rarely, if ever, eaten raw. Saltwater eels are simmered until soft and the bones are no longer a hard enough to post an annoyance. The liquid it has cooked in is mixed with soy sauce, sugar, and rice wine, and then reduced. This then accompanies the eel as a sauce. Soy sauce is not eaten with the eel.

Salmon Roe (Ikura)

Salmon roe is a type of fish egg. The small orange spherical eggs taste slightly of salmon and are rich and sweet. When served as part of a sushi course, the salmon roe is prepared by separating the eggs from the membrane they are contained in and soaking them in soy sauce and rice wine. This improves the texture of the salmon roe by making it smooth and light.

Flying Fish Roe (Tobiko)

These fish eggs are very small, much smaller than

Salmon roe, and are naturally a reddish orange color. However, sometimes they are colored with various ingredients and may be black, green, or yellow. If you like spicy food, try the green kind as nigiri, it is colored with wasabi and is can be very intense.

Sea Urchin Roe (Uni)

Sea urchin roe refers to the gonad organ of a sea urchin. Uni is sourced from both male and female sea urchins, with not much difference in flavor or color between the two. Both are yellow or orange and taste rich and creamy.

Sushi History: During World War II, food was scarce in Japan and the military had imposed strict rationing. A popular street food at the time was nigirizushi, which contained fresh fish caught locally that was marinated in vinegar or sake, or slightly cooked for preservation. Rice and fish were hard to get, and as the war continued on, one by one the sushi street stalls closed. Sushi chefs left the major cities to set up shop in the provinces. After World War II, the occupying American military forced the remaining sushi street vendors to move indoors to more sanitary conditions. Because rice and fish continued to be tightly regulated (each sushi could only contain a specified amount of rice and fish), sushi chefs began to substitute other toppings. They began to experiment with things like mullet, toxic puffer fish, and clams; they added pickled vegetables, mushrooms and gourd shavings, all of which resulted in a sushi creation much like the sushi we love today. This period in sushi's history is when sushi shifted from being predominantly a street food to becoming the dining experience we are familiar with today.

Lesson 4
Maki

Sushi is not really about flavor as much
as texture. Everything is usually
made bite size so you can eat it in
one bite, which is more proper.
-Tim Hoffman

Makizushi translates to "rolled sushi." Maki is comprised of one or more fillings wrapped in a layer of sushi rice, which is rolled in a sheet of nori (seaweed) into a cylinder shape. Because the outer makizushi is wrapped in nori, it may also be called *nori-makizushi*. The cylinder is shaped by rolling with a bamboo mat, using gentle pressure to bond the ingredients. It is then sliced into six or eight pieces and served. The ingredients used include many that were described in the previous lesson, plus various fruits and vegetables.

Futomaki

Futomaki, or "fat" rolls, are known for their large size, usually two inches or more in diameter, as well as their beauty when sliced. The highly colorful fillings are chosen as much for their visual appeal as for their flavor. Chefs strive to combine ingredients that bring together just the right balance of tastes, mingling the sweet and the salty with the sour and the tangy. Sometimes vegetarian, futomaki may also have seafood fillings (like chopped tuna or whitefish) and are constructed in the same way as other rolled sushi, with the fillings wrapped in rice and then nori. Skilled chefs can arrange the ingredients in just such a way so that when sliced, the sushi resembles images like a star, a sunrise, or a flower. Futomaki are usually eaten in slices, but there is an exception. During a special Japanese festival that marks the beginning of a new season, the futomaki is eaten in an unsliced roll as part of the festival ritual. It is thought to usher in good luck throughout the upcoming season.

Hosomaki

Hosomaki is a popular form of makizushi. Meaning "thin rolls," these sliced pieces are about one inch in diameter and usually contain only one filling, common examples are tuna roll and cucumber roll. They are served as snacks or, depending upon the filling, may be used as a palate cleanser between raw fish and other courses. Hosomaki uses half a sheet of nori and a bit thinner layer of sushi rice. Some chefs place shiso leaves, an Asian minty herb, between the filling and the rice, which makes a beautiful bright green contrast design. You may have seen a shiso leaf in the past—they commonly make an elegant presentation on sushi dishes as a natural bowl to hold grated wasabi. Others may use scallions between the seafood and the rice. Because the ingredients are so simple, hosomaki lends itself well to flavorful cuts like tuna and yellowtail. And because the design is simple as well, chefs don't worry so much about how the slices look and are able to use trimmings and pieces of leftover seafood as a way of economizing. Hosomaki is sliced and served as with other types of maki, cutting a roll into 6-8 pieces.

Uramaki

Uramaki, meaning "inside out roll," is especially popular in Western sushi restaurants.The fillings are wrapped directly in nori and the rice is wrapped on the outside. With uramaki, the rice is laid directly on the bamboo mat and the nori is laid atop the rice. Usually just 1 to 3 fillings are placed at one end of the nori, and the nori is rolled with the rice on the outside. The roll is then coated with toasted sesame seeds, red fish roe, or some other topping; the sticky rice is perfect for holding onto the coatings. The uramaki is then sliced in the traditional method and served. Some chefs add an additional topping on top of the slices such as a sauce, black sesame seeds, diced vegetables, additional slices of fish, or Flying Fish Roe.

The California roll and its variations is a type of uramaki that most people have seen at some point. The California roll is often the non-sushi lover's first roll. When people are ready to go out on a limb and try sushi for the first time, they usually go for the California roll. The roll, a type of uramaki, is constructed from the inside out and is made of crab meat (sometimes imitation), avocado, and cucumber and then is sprinkled with sesame seeds.

Temaki

Temaki, or "hand rolls," are a fun option for sushi beginners. For temaki, sushi rice, and fillings are loosely rolled into a four inch long nori cone using the hands—no bamboo mat is used. A half sheet of nori is placed in the palm of one hand and a small scoop of rice is added to the center, then spread with the fingers in a thin layer across half the sheet. Any other ingredients desired can be added and laid diagonally across the sushi rice. The nori is then folded into a cone shape and rolled tightly. You end up with what looks like an ice cream cone of sushi. These large rolls are meant to be picked up and eaten with one's hands. Rarely found on the menus of formal Japanese restaurants, temaki is becoming very popular among Westerners both at casual restaurants and as a make-at-home item.

Vegetarian Sushi

For vegetarians who want to join their friends at the local sushi shop or make sushi at home, maki is the best option. As with the California roll, this is very much a Western creation, but many different fruits and vegetables can be cut into strips and rolled into sushi. Mango, asparagus, peppers, avocado, spinach, cucumber, carrots, zucchini, and celery are commonly used in vegetarian sushi rolls.

Sushi History: Spicy sushi is commonly enhanced with intense flavors and spices like Japanese mayonnaise, Sriracha sauce, wasabi, or chili oil. Whether drizzled atop the sushi or inside with the other ingredients, these spices and sauces may be used to disguise the flavor of less desirable or older cuts of seafood. Spicy rolls, such as the common spicy tuna roll, a type of uramaki, started out as a way to use the odd pieces of meat leftover from sashimi and other sushi that requires excellent presentation. The leftover pieces of meat are combined with chili paste, and other ingredients, sometimes including crunchy bits of tempura, and wrapped up in a roll.

Lesson 5
Other Types

I've been making sushi for 38 years, and I'm still learning. You have to consider the size and color of the ingredients, how much salt and vinegar to use and how the seasons affect the fattiness of the fish.
-Masaharu Morimoto

The following are some of the more unusual types of sushi that are more likely to be found in Japan than other countries. If you're planning a trip to Japan, you may want to make sure you're able to try some of these exotic and unusual types of sushi.

Oshi

Oshizushi is less popular in the United States than it is internationally, and yet it is some of the most different and unique sushi out there. Originating in Osaka, oshi (meaning "pressed") is made by pressing the fermented rice and fish together using wooden compresses. The sushi is prepared with the nori in delicate combinations and then pressed, which better combines the flavors and textures. Oshi is faster to prepare than regular rolls, which enables the chef to explore more exotic and artistic designs. Many of the forms of oshi are specially shaped to be dipped in wasabi and enjoyed after being cut into pieces for easy consumption. One thing about oshizushi that's different from other types is that it is made with fermented rice and has a very distinct flavor, which is either loved or hated depending upon the taste buds of the diner.

There are many different varieties of oshi; a few of the most well known are:

Hazushi oshi, sometimes seen written as *kaki-no-ha zushi*, is a specialty of the Japanese city of Nara. It's made using salted mackerel or salmon that is placed on sushi rice, then wrapped in persimmon leaves and pressed. The persimmon leaves give it a mellow flavor and aroma and preserve the sushi, enabling it to last a very long time. Visitors to Nara often buy hazushi to take home as gifts to family and friends.

Hakozushi oshi, or "box" sushi, is made by pressing layers of sushi rice and a variety of ingredients into a wooden box-like press, then removing the top and sides of the box and slicing the sushi into squares or rectangles. The sushi pieces are then beautifully arranged in a box for serving. The layer ingredients include delectable flavors and textures like: thinly sliced, sweetened and salty shiitake mushrooms; toasted nori (seaweed); sea eel; red shrimp alongside yellow omelet; and crimson sea bream. Hakozushi is popular in lunch boxes for a sophisticated lunch.

Battera is a type of ochi similar to hakozushi in the method in which it is prepared, excepting that batterra is made upside down. It begins with a layer of aspidistra leaves (inedible leaves that make it easier to remove the wooden press) that is followed by a fish layer, usually salted gizzard shad or mackerel (both of which have a strong, oily flavor), and then is topped with sushi rice. Once pressed, the entire loaf is flipped over and easily removed from the mold. Depending upon the seafood, the batterra is cut into squares or rectangles, or it may be sliced like a pie. An especially beautiful pie shaped design is created when boiled shrimp are used for the seafood layer and the ochi is prepared in a round cake-like pan. The shrimp are arranged in a radiating circle pattern, topped with rice and sometimes nori, then pressed, flipped and sliced in wedges.

Chirashi

Chirashizushi (meaning "scattered") is a type of sushi that is a one-dish meal; very easy to make and very filling. It's a bed of rice with a variety of toppings, called gu, that may or may not include seafood. Chirashi is not as popular in the United States as it is in other parts of the world. Traditionally, Japanese rice is used for the rice, but the chirashi rice recipe calls for more vinegar and less sugar than traditional sushi rice. Chirashi can vary quite a bit from one chef to the next considering the cornucopia of toppings one might add (commonly nine different toppings), which are frequently chosen for their pleasing appearance as much as for their flavor.

The assortment of toppings enables the diner to sample a large variety of fish and vegetables. The rice bed is compacted so that it doesn't break apart easily, but not so much so that it is difficult to eat.

Chirashi is often sold in lunchboxes by Japanese street vendors as a fast food. There are several different types of chirashi, such as: barazushi and tekonezushi that mix the toppings into the rice; mushizushi, which is preferred in the winter, served warm and steamed; and sakezushi, which is seasoned with sake and fermented slightly before serving.

Nare

Narezushi was actually originally the process of preserving fish (pressing the fish between layers of salt and allowing to ferment over several months). Narezushi (meaning "fermented"), is one of the oldest traditional sushi dishes as well as one of the rarest. Considered to be a delicacy, the shelf life of narezushi is somewhere in the range of three years. It continues to be very popular in many areas of Japan. Using whichever fish is most available or regional, the fish is filleted and heavily salted, stuffed with rice, and left to pickle for 40 to 50 days in fermenting rice, during which time the desired flavor is reached and the bones have become soft. Some regions add vegetables as well. The resulting strong-tasting narezushi has a sour flavor not often appreciated outside of Japan.

The long complex process of preparing narezushi is a tradition that has been maintained for centuries by families in the fishing villages of the Province of Wakasa. Unfortunately, few people of the younger generations are interested in learning the techniques or carrying on the tradition, and the production of narezushi has become increasingly rare.

Funa

Funazushi is a rare type of narezushi that is made from the funa fish, which is a type of carp native to Lake Biwa in the Shiga Prefecture. In the past, the first funazushi of the season was offered to the gods as a gift, as rice was considered a divine food and funa fish were thought to be guardians of the rice paddy. Today, the funa fish population is in decline, suspected to be a result of changes in the ecosystem of Biwa Lake. In an attempt to continue production, producers tried substituting other fish but found the altered taste to be unacceptable. Others stopped making funazushi altogether. Despite problems with the funa population, some families have continued to produce funazushi for many generations, sometimes taking pre-orders in years when the funa supply is low. One renowned family is the Kitamuras, who have specialized in funazushi for almost 400 years.

Funazushi is made by salt curing fresh caught funa then pickling it with cooked rice. The fresh fish is cleaned, leaving the ovaries intact, stuffed with salt, and then packed in more salt, and aged for up to two years. After salt curing, the funa is rinsed and dried in the sun. The fish and rice are then arranged in layers in a deep wooden barrel, the barrel is closed and a heavy weight is positioned on top. The Kitamuras are very particular about the rice they use; where it's grown and the manner in which it has been dried and harvested. The rice pickling stage typically adds another year to the process, after which the funazushi is pickled once again in a new bed of rice, taking the whole process to approximately three years. The finished dish has an over-powering aroma and a very sharp and vinegary taste, somewhat cheese-like, with the rice rich and creamy like a porridge. Some say it tastes exactly the way it smells.

Sushi History: One ancient myth about the creation of sushi says that an old woman, fearing that a pot of rice she had was about to be stolen by bandits, hid it in a tree near an osprey nest. When she recovered her rice, it had started to ferment and was covered by fish scraps. Tasting it, she found it was delicious and had helped to preserve the fish.

Lesson 6
Accoutrements

Fifteen years ago, people were making jokes
about sushi being bait, and now, in parts of
L.A. -- not in Japanese neighborhoods
at all, especially on the West side --
it seems like there's a little sushi bar
in almost every mini-mall.
-Russ Parsons, Journalist

Moist Towel (Oshibori)

Giving guests a moist towel to wash their hands
and face is an old tradition in Japan. Today many
Japanese restaurants provide a small towel for their

guests as soon as they are seated. Traditionally the towels are cold in the summer and warm in the winter.

Chopsticks (Hashi)

As mentioned previously, it is common for nigiri sushi to be picked up with your hand, but for everything else you'll be using chopsticks. If you have never used chopsticks before don't worry, no one is good with them the first time, but you can learn in a few minutes. Give it a try and don't ask for a fork instead. Your server or whoever you are eating with will probably be happy to teach you this skill.

If you are using wooden chopsticks, after you break them apart, do not rub them together to remove splinters. This is considered rude. The only practical reason for people rubbing their chopsticks together is when eating noodle dishes; some people rub them together to make a rougher surface on the end of the chopsticks to make it easier to pick up the noodles.

Soy Sauce (Shōyu)

This is a fermented mix of soybeans and brine,

which is aged to allow for months and then forms a paste. Following the fermentation, the paste is then pressed into a juice. This juice is used to form the basis for soy sauce, an ancient condiment which has been a part of the sushi experience. Soy Sauce, called *shōyu* or *murasaki*, in sushi bar slang, is more complex topic than you are probably expecting. In Asian nations, soy sauce is available in a complex array of varieties, however in a sushi bar you will usually have a sold, black sauce and you will be given a small, shallow bowl to pour some soy sauce into. Throughout the meal, as needed, you can dip your pieces of sushi or sashimi into the soy sauce in this bowl. Don't feel like you need to drown your food in the soy sauce though, a little bit is plenty, and some types, especially the more complex maki rolls, do not need any extra soy sauce.

Wasabi

True wasabi is made from the root of the Wasabia japonica plant, and is traditionally ground to a paste with the use of a sharkskin grater. However, the environment needed to grow the wasabia plant is very difficult to find outside a few select areas of Japan, so it is quite expensive and rare in other parts of the world. The pile of green "wasabi" that you find at your local sushi bar will most likely be colored horseradish, which is fine, just keep in mind that you should try the real stuff if you get the chance.

Many Western sushi eaters, who are used to spicy foods, go overboard with the wasabi, some even going so far as to make a paste with their wasabi and soy sauce to dip their sushi in. This really takes away from the subtle flavors you should be experiencing with your sushi. For the most part, you can expect your sushi chef to include the right amount of wasabi in each piece.

Ginger (Gari)

Ginger is used to assist in the digestion of food and with sushi it is also used as a palate cleanser. Typically, sushi will be served with a small pile of ginger that has been sliced thin and pickled in vinegar. Eat a slice or two a few times throughout the meal, especially when switching between different types of sushi, to cleanse your palate.

Sushi History: Nobuyuki Matsuhia, known to the world as Nobu, is a master chef with restaurants stretching over three continents. His unique style, known as Nobu stlye, was influenced by his years in Peru, where he absorbed the culture and incorporated it into traditional Japanese dishes. His creations of contrasting and unexpected ingredients have earned him many culinary awards and accolades. After finishing high school in Japan, he began his training, spending years busing tables, washing dishes, and cleaning until finally becoming a chef. Nobu's career spans many years of hard work and determination, from Japan to Peru to Argentina to Alaska, where a fire destroyed his restaurant and left him financially ruined. Nobu went on to open another restaurant in Beverly Hills nine years later, which is where he met Robert Di Nero. In 1994, he and Di Nero opened Nobu New York, which was followed in the years to come by restaurants all over the world. Today, Nobu Matsuhisa is a much respected celebrity chef and restaurateur who takes pride in the artistry of his dishes, insisting upon using only the finest ingredients and providing flawless service.

Lesson 7
Food Pairing

Kids are now eating things like edamame and sushi. I didn't know what shiitake mushrooms were when I was 10 - most kids today do.
-Emeril Lagasse, Chef

Miso Soup

Miso soup is made of a traditional stock called dashi, with a miso paste mixed in. The miso paste is made by fermenting soybeans, rice, or barley, with salt and a the *kōji* fungus, then aging for several months. The process results in a wonderfully flavorful paste which ranges in intensity and color, as well as in variations by region. The dashi stock is commonly made from shitake mushrooms, katsuobushi (block of fermented fish), dried kelp, or baby sardines. The shitake and kelp dashis make excellent vegetarian style soup bases. Western style miso soup is often made by combining miso paste with a vegetable broth and daikon radish, which is a mild flavored white radish.

Tofu and vegetables are added to miso soup as the solid component, with some floating atop and some sinking to the bottom. The choices are meant to offset and complement one another in terms of color and contrast, of texture and flavor. Vegetables of choice generally reflect the seasons and are balanced in flavor; strong against subtle. Nutritionally, miso soup is very high in sodium but is an excellent source of fiber, protein, vitamin E, vitamin B12 (which is a vegan favorite), and other protective fatty acids.

Seaweed Salad (Wakame)

Sometimes listed on menus as "seaweed salad," wakame is a dark green stringy seaweed, slightly sweet in flavor. In the 1960s, wakame began to appear in the United States in natural food and

Asian grocery stores as an offshoot of the macrobiotic movement. In the 1970s, the popularity of Japanese restaurants and the emergence of sushi further increased consumer awareness and demand. Wakame is sold fresh and refrigerated, frozen, or dried. If dried, the wakame has to be rehydrated by soaking for ten minutes or so.

Green Salad

Many Japanese-style restaurants offer a green salad with an excellent ginger dressing. The ginger dressing is usually a combination of fresh minced ginger, onions, garlic, celery, rice vinegar, oil, and a few other tangy and tart ingredients that are liquefied in a blender and chilled to perfection. Some chefs add fresh carrot to the blend as well, which gives the dressing a deep orange color.

Edamame

Edamame is a young specialty soybean, which is hand picked and generally consumed as a vegetable or snack. Edamame is easily prepared by boiling or steaming the beans as they come with a bit of sea salt, which is recommended because of its enhancing marine flavor. Full of organic compounds, amino acids, fiber, and protein, they can be consumed hot or cold and make an excellent sushi pairing choice for vegetarians in particular.

To eat edamame, make certain that you bite the pod and suck out the seeds. Do not consume the pod, as it will be thick and difficult to consume. Soybeans, when they grow older, are used as the fundamental basis for many other food production items. However, this is the case after they are made hard and inconsumable to the average person as an appetizer. Edamame has become a very popular dish in restaurants all over the world and is often served in place of Miso Soup or different salads as well.

Sashimi

As mentioned previously, sashimi is not a type of sushi because it does not include sushi rice, however sashimi is almost always served with a meal that includes sushi. Sashimi consists of fresh fish, almost always served raw, sliced thinly. An order of sashimi usually includes 4-8 pieces of fish, depending on the restaurant. To eat sashimi you simply pick up a piece of the fish with your chopsticks, dip it in soy sauce (if you prefer), and place the whole thing in your mouth. As with nigiri, avoid trying to bite off just part of the piece of fish and putting the rest down.

Sashimi is traditionally served at the beginning of the meal, before sushi, to ensure the diner is most receptive to its subtle flavors and textures of the raw fish by itself, this is also a great way to gauge the quality of the fish before you eat the sushi. In practice today however, especially outside of Japan, most people simply order sushi and sashimi together and do not follow any strict rules about what order they eat the different types. Sashimi is often garnished with daikon radishes that are sliced into long thin strips. This garnish is meant to be consumed along with the sashimi. The most common types of sashimi are salmon and tuna.

The word "sashimi" is also used to describe the quality of the fish, as in "sashimi grade fish," which simply means that it is fresh and has been preserved in a way so that it is ok to be consumed raw. If you try making sushi at home that includes raw fish, make sure you are using sashimi grade fish from a reliable fish merchant. The online resources page includes links to some of the top online merchants and more information about selecting good fish:

27Press.com/sushi

One rare form of sashimi is also one of the most infamous: *fugu*, which means "river pig." Fugu is a dish made from the liver of the Japanese fugu pufferfish. Fugu is reported to have a delicate taste paired with a tingling sensation. It's considered a special delicacy in Japan and can cost as much as $400 per serving. Fugu organs contain an extremely fatal poison, and fugu is considered one of the most lethal dishes in the world. Japan allows only certified chefs to prepare this dish, and it is the one food that the Japanese Emperor is forbidden to consume.

The certification process involves two to three years of training and many extensive exams that focus on attention to detail and safety. Before earning a special license, the chef must pass a practical exam in which he consumes the fugu he has prepared himself. Fugu is usually presented in an highly ornate fashion and is expected to be eaten by itself, with no side dishes.

Dining on fugu can indeed be serious business; there is no known cure for its deadly toxin. The poison is cruel, paralyzing the victim while completely conscious and ending with death from asphyxiation. Even a small amount is capable of killing an adult. Roughly 50 people a year die as a result of fugu poisoning. The sale of fugu is completely forbidden in Europe, and it is only allowed to be imported to the United States for the handful of Japanese restaurants that are certified to prepare it.

Outlawed in Australia and Germany, *ikizukuri* is a very controversial type of sashimi that is made from living seafood. Ikizukuri, which means "prepared alive," is primarily made from fish, but squid, eel, octopus, shrimp, or lobster may also be used. Often restaurants display seafood in large tanks from which the customer may choose their entree. The fish is carefully filleted without killing it, exposing its still beating heart, gills that continue to gasp for air, and moving eyes. The sashimi is then artfully arranged on or around the still live body and served with colorful pickled vegetables and seaweed.

Animal rights groups protest ikizukuri, claiming that it is cruel and unnecessary torture of animals that can feel pain and experience fear. Supporters feel ikizukuri is part of the Japanese heritage and culture, they view it as an act of embracing ones food sources and appreciating the sacrifice of the live animal as opposed to distancing oneself from the live animal as Westerners do.

Sushi History: Umami, which means "pleasant savory taste" in Japanese, is one of the five known elements of taste (salty, sweet, sour, bitter, and umami). Though difficult to describe, it has a mild meaty taste that lingers on the tongue and induces a mouthwatering sensation that can be felt in the mouth and down into the throat. Not palatable by itself, umami balances and rounds the flavors of a dish. Fermented fish sauces, dashi (Japanese soup stock), and shitake mushrooms all carry the umami taste, as well as seafood, cured meats and some fruits and vegetables like tomatoes, Chinese cabbage, and spinach. Umami is said to increase the intensity of two lesser ingredients when combined, especially when enhanced by aroma. The taste "umami" was first coined in 1908 by Dr. Ikeda of Tokyo Imperial University who intended to commercialize it as a seasoning. He wanted to identify exactly what it was that gave kombu seaweed its pleasant taste. Learning that kombu's distinctive flavor came from its monosodium glutamate (MSG), he went on to invent a method of extracting and crystallizing the MSG. Despite many anecdotal reports of MSG consumption causing odd symptoms, no real evidence has ever been found that MSG actually causes any side effects.

Lesson 8
Drink Pairing

It is the man who drinks the first bottle of sake; then the second bottle drinks the first, and finally it is the sake that drinks the man.
-Japanese proverb

Green Tea

Tea has been popular in Japan for at least 1,000 years, and while Japan remains a major production center for green tea, most of it stays within the country. What you normally find at sushi restaurants is basic Chinese green tea, often *sencha*. While some consider green tea (called *agari* in sushi bar slang) an end of meal drink, it's an excellent beverage to accompany the meal as well.

It is an excellent beverage to pair with sushi if your goal is simply to enjoy the sushi itself. It cleanses the palate and quenches the thirst that the vinegar in the rice can arouse, allowing you to concentrate on the subtle flavors of the sushi. Green tea is usually served very hot. When you order green tea in a sushi restaurant it is usually brought out to you in a large pot with a small cup that you can refill yourself as much as you want.

19 Lessons On Tea by 27Press is an excellent resource to learn more about buying, brewing, and drinking the best tea.

Sake

It is thought that sake originated as a sacred drink; virgins would chew on rice and spit it into a bowl to begin the fermentation process. Unfortunately, modern health standards do not allow this specific brewing technique to continue, but modern sake is still an amazing, complex, and diverse category of alcoholic beverage. Though sake is sometimes referred to as rice wine, its production method is more like beer, which converts starch to sugar to alcohol, while wine is produced directly from fermenting natural fruit sugars to alcohol. There are several distinct types of sake and some are meant to be served cold, or hot, or even room temperature depending on the type. A bottle of sake will typically have recommended serving instructions. The alcohol content usually ranges from 18-21%. Since sake is made from rice, many Japanese people consider drinking sake at the same time as they eat sushi to be redundant, like eating a sandwich with a side of bread. It is traditional to drink sake before or after a meal involving rice, but not during.

Wine

Wine made from grapes is not a common choice to go with sushi, but some people prefer it. Sommeliers generally recommend either white or sparkling wines to go with your sushi.

Beer

Beer is the alcoholic beverage of choice in Japan, accounting for almost two-thirds of alcohol consumption on the islands, which might help to explain why beer is probably the best and most widely suggested accompaniment to sushi. Most sushi restaurants have several Japanese beers available, including ones from Asahi, Kirin, Sapporo, and others, all of which pair excellently with a typical sushi meal. For non-Japanese beer, any good pilsner will also go well with your sushi.

The online resources guide to this book contains more extensive articles about sushi and drink pairing:

27Press.com/sushi

Sushi History: Green tea was brought to Japan from China in 1191 by a Buddhist priest known as Zen Master Eisai. He founded Japan's first Zen Buddhist temple in the Kyushu region, and it was here his monks cultivated Japan's first green tea. This became the most famed green tea in all of Japan, and from Kyushu, seeds and cultivation methods were spread to Kyoto and other regions. The southern region of Japan, just south of Kyoto, remains Japan's premier growing region for green tea.

Lesson 9
The Meal

In order to make delicious food, you must eat delicious food. The quality of ingredients is important, but one must develop a palate capable of discerning good and bad.
-Jiro Ono, Sushi Shokunin

Bar vs Table

If you are going into a restaurant for the first time part of what you decide will be to sit at the sushi bar or to sit at a table. Always sit at the bar if you can, the sushi chef will usually give preferential treatment to customers sitting at the sushi bar as opposed to those out in the dining area, and you may even be rewarded with a free appetizer just for sitting at the bar. The sushi bar is intended to be a communal, social event among customers and the chef. You will be able to see the selection of ingredients at the bar. It is important to remember to only order sushi items from the chef and to order all other drinks and items from your server.

It is also more acceptable to order small amounts, sashimi first, at a time while at the bar. If you sit at the bar you will quickly see that the atmosphere will be less formal and you will get to watch the chefs at work with their magic as they prepare amazing and colorful creations right in front of you. If you sit at the bar the dynamic will be less formal, it is ok to ask the chef a few questions about their craft but make sure that you do not monopolize the chef's time with questions as he can quickly get backed up on orders. Plus, you will get your food at the perfect temperature, the fish will be cold and the rice will be warm, each plate will be handed directly to you as soon as the chef is done with it.

If you like surprises, is considered a compliment to leave your entire meal up to the whims of the chef, and it almost guarantees you'll get the freshest pieces. This is called omakase, and you are saying you are entrusting your meal to the chef. Usually you discuss a set price beforehand and the chef makes whatever he thinks is best for your meal for that price. This will likely include sushi, sashimi, and other small Japanese dishes, such as soup. You may not like everything, but it is an excellent way to try new things and get the freshest ingredients.

If you are feeling less adventurous or you have several people with you, you may prefer to be seated at a table in the restaurant. You will order all drinks and food items, including your sushi, from the server. Many restaurants encourage patrons seated at tables to order all of their sushi at one time by marking their selections on a paper menu that is handed in to the sushi chef. Descriptions of different kinds of rolls offered by the restaurant are usually printed on the main menu.

A newer trend in the sushi industry is restaurants that have conveyor belts which run throughout the restaurant. The customers simply pick up the plates they want off the belt and are charged at the end for what they have eaten. This is not yet common outside Japan.

Etiquette

The following are a few more bits of information to keep in mind when eating sushi.

If you are moving a piece of sushi from one plate to another using chopsticks, even for yourself, flip your chopsticks around and use the ends you are not eating with to do this. Not doing this is considered rude. Also, do not hand a piece of sushi off from one pair of chopsticks to another.

Avoid adding too much soy sauce or wasabi to your sushi, and don't make a paste by mixing the two together. This is not a contest to see who can eat the hottest meal, and could be taken as an insult to the chef. The chef has already added the right amount of wasabi and sometimes soy sauce as well. So a slight dip in your bowl of soy sauce, if you prefer, is usually all that's needed before eating a piece of sushi; enjoy the subtle flavors and textures of the rice and fish.

Eat everything you order. In Japanese culture it is very rude to leave anything uneaten. If you're not sure how much you want, remember that it is acceptable to place more than one order during the course of the meal; order a little, enjoy it, then order more later.

During traditional Japanese meals, people do not

pour their own drinks, the participants take turns pouring each others drinks when they see someone's glass getting low.

Sushi History: Since 2005, Tyson Cole has become a prominent figure in the sushi world. He started his career in the 1990s when he was simply looking for any job he could find and ended up with a dishwasher job in a Japanese restaurant in Austin, TX. He became interested in making sushi and eventually become an apprentice in Austin and learned Japanese. Eventually he opened his restaurant Uchi, and has since opened several more. Tyson is an excellent example of how an American, who grew up with no connection to Japanese culture, can now become a respected sushi master. In an interview in the documentary *Sushi: The Global Catch*, Tyson says, "I've kinda defined Uchi food as my food, and my food stays true to the Japanese aesthetic, but not traditional Japanese; so applying new techniques, new ingredients, new styles, and making sense of them, and how they can go together."

Lesson 10
Sushi Chef Training

All I want to do is make better sushi.
-Jiro Ono, Sushi Shokunin

Itamae is the Japanese word for chef, which translated means "in front of the cutting board." Master sushi chefs are referred to as sushi shokunin, meaning "skilled professionals." The chef who stands in front of the cutting board is traditionally the head chef, in charge of the kitchen and all sushi preparation, etiquette, and technique. The itamae may also be responsible for accommodating the guests, establishing a courteous and congenial atmosphere, and handling any pricing determinations. Becoming a sushi chef is a long and difficult process that requires learning many skills. A good sushi chef must be knowledgeable in all areas of Japanese cuisine.

Sushi Chef Training in Japan

The process of becoming a sushi chef in Japan is strenuous; the training is steeped in tradition and the teachings of all the masters who have gone before. Though it is not required that he be of Japanese descent, it is mandatory that all chefs undergo the same rigorous training. Part of the job involves cooking as a performance. Meals are often prepared with the chef positioned in front of the diner, so a good sushi chef must be comfortable and competent slicing, dicing, and serving directly before the diner's table.

The profession, which upholds such ancient samurai ideals as strict self-discipline and high personal standards, is considered an honor and deeply respected. Sushi chefs are incredibly dedicated to their work and very serious about their personal appearance and presentation skills. Traditionally, the sushi chef wears a spotless uniform of a white hat, white coat and white apron, with a carbon-steel, extremely sharp, knife carried in a sheath about the waist. It's no surprise that the knives cost hundreds of dollars each and are meticulously cared for, much like samurai swords, cleaned frequently throughout the day and sharpened before and after each use.

Most Japanese sushi chefs go through a fifteen year process. A future itamae's apprenticeship is as much about learning food preparation skills as it is about demonstrating dedication to the art. Professional sushi chefs must not only master sushi rice and properly prepared sushi-grade seafood, they must also become expert in other Japanese dishes as well, such as udon (a type of noodle), tempura (battered and fried seafood or vegetables), and more. By the time their training is finished, these individuals possess a well-rounded set of Japanese culinary skills. It takes years of training and apprenticeship to achieve the expertise to call oneself a sushi chef.

A typical timeline for a sushi chef's training is as follows:

In the first year, the trainee is simply a kitchen apprentice, sweeping and washing floors, cleaning dishes and other odd jobs. In the second year, the trainee becomes familiar with the preparation of small shellfish such as clams. In the third and fourth years of study, trainees are promoted to preparing staff meals; this role is known as a shikomi, which means "preparation." The fifth year of training is spent learning the intricacies and nuances of preparing the sushi rice. Once the trainee satisfactorily learns to prepare the rice, he is promoted to wakita, which means "beside the cutting board," and his training focuses on learning how to prepare fresh vegetables and seafood. In the sixth year, trainees are allowed to work behind a sushi bar, serving less complicated takeout sushi rolls. This continues throughout years seven, eight and nine, as the sushi chef-in-training gains experience working with customers. After a decade of training, the title of itamae has finally been earned, along with the right to stand in front of the cutting board. The chef will continue working in the restaurant where he gained his training for another five years. After fifteen years of apprenticeship, study and hard work, the sushi chef takes his place at the head of the kitchen.

In the documentary *Jiro Dreams of Sushi*, Jiro Ono says the following, which provides a glimpse into the mindset of a sushi shokunin, "Once you decide on your occupation you must immerse yourself in your work. You have to fall in love with your work. Never complain about your job. You must dedicate your life to mastering your skill.

That's the secret of success and is the key to being regarded honorably."

Outside Japan

Outside of Japan, the path to becoming a sushi chef is not as rigid; there are several options for training.

One way is to simply get a job of any kind at a Japanese restaurant that will allow the future chef to eventually help with simple food preparation, then to start learning the basics and eventually be trained on more complex tasks until they are making food for customers. Along the way, the person will need to find a good mentor to work with and train them in the skills required to be a sushi chef. The chef will need to spend many hours practicing on their own as well.

There are also sushi schools. This is probably the best option for someone in The United States who wants to become a sushi chef. The student can learn all the basics in school and then go on to an internship, or perhaps right into a chef's job, or possibly work in Japan for a few years. These schools offer courses that usually last several months, cost a few thousand dollars to enroll, and are taught by sushi professionals. They include a well-defined program for teaching students the skills they need to know to start working in a sushi restaurant.

If you are interested in learning more about this, the previously mentioned book *The Story of Sushi* by Trevor Corson follows a group of students during a semester at one of these schools in 2005. It provides an excellent in-depth look at the the training and discipline involved in making sushi. Also, if you would like to get a little professional training in how to make sushi but don't want to enroll in the full program, some of the schools offer shorter programs that last only a few days, as well as offering private lessons.

Whichever option is chosen, many non-Japanese sushi chefs will also choose to work in Japan for a few years to improve their skills. Non-Japanese people who are trying to become sushi chefs also find it important to commit to learning the Japanese language to provide a more authentic experience for the customers in the sushi bars where they work.

Our online resources includes a list of the best sushi schools:
27Press.com/sushi

Sushi History: Historically, only men have been allowed to be sushi chefs, and this is basically still the case in Japan today. However, outside of Japan, especially as more non-Japanese people started opening sushi restaurants, more women have entered the profession. The reason most often given why women cannot be sushi chefs is that they have warmer hands, which will make the rice and fish too warm. This is not true though; women's hands are actually slightly cooler than men's. Other common excuses given include: wearing perfume, not being physically strong enough, and having smaller hands.

Lesson 11
Making Sushi

One of my favorite things to make is homemade sushi. I know how to make the rolls and it's really fun to do.
-Carly Rae Jepsen, Musician

Making sushi at home can be a fun and rewarding experience. Do not think that you cannot prepare sushi at home just because you are not a trained itamae. The key is to have a good time and don't expect perfection on your first few tries.

Note that the following lessons are not thorough instructions so much as an outline of what is to be expected when making sushi. It will be beneficial to use more detailed instructions and recipes when preparing sushi for the first time.

Getting Organized

It is best to be prepared before you begin constructing your sushi and have everything you are going to need organized in a common area of the kitchen. Cleanliness is as important as creativity to ensure that all goes smoothly and efficiently. You may also choose to wear gloves.

In order to prepare the different parts of the sushi, there are a few basic things you will need:

- Sushi rice.
- Your fish and other ingredients.
- Sharp knives.
- Nori (seaweed sheets).
- Bamboo mat (or *maki su*) for rolling the sushi.

Buying Ingredients

The first consideration must be about your ingredients; don't skimp on quality ingredients for sushi. Here are a few tips and tricks to assist in shopping for ingredients:

Decide what rolls you are going to make.

Choose easy rolls for your first few ventures. Remember, you are not a professional sushi chef and no one is expecting you to be. Start out simple with something like a tuna or salmon roll, or perhaps a California roll. This will ensure that you are able to make the sushi easily without too many ingredients, making just a few varieties in the proper way.

If you make it too complicated the first few times, you may get discouraged. Simple recipes will streamline the process and produce equally delicious results, while providing a satisfying sense of accomplishment for the novice sushi chef!

Shop only at the best locations for ingredients and make certain that you observe all correct temperature requirements. If using raw fish or other seafood in your preparation, you must be certain that it is of sashimi grade and has been stored and handled properly from the fishing boat to your counter top.

Nori

The Asian section of your grocery store will have a large selection of nori. The best choice is organic nori, which is healthier, more authentic, and will better hold up in the rolling process because it is thicker. In general, look for a dark brownish-black or purple color, which indicates good quality. You may choose to enhance the flavor of the nori by passing the glossy side over a flame 2-3 times from a safe distance, or by toasting over a gas or electric burner. You just want to heat it for a few seconds, don't overheat; remove from the heat when the color changes. This makes the nori easier to chew, gives it a crisp texture, and brings out the flavor and aroma. If you should need to cut the nori sheet, use scissors, or a knife pressing down through the sheet on a cutting board.

Seafood

Research which location in your area carries the freshest seafood. If you cannot find it at a grocery store, consider going to a farmers market to ensure that you are able to get the best fish from a local source. Avoid genetically modified fish to ensure you are getting quality fish as well as fish without any unnatural enhancements.

Rice

The rice used to make sushi rice is not the same as other generic white rice. It is a special kind of rice, called Japanese white-hulled sushi rice, and if at all possible, it's usually best to purchase your rice from an Asian grocery store. Sushi rice has a shiny, rounded grain, and high quality rice will have very few broken grains.

There are many sushi rice recipes available, all listing basically the same ingredients as listed in the section in Lesson 1, with slight variations in quantities and preparation styles. You will need to experiment a little before settling on your perfect sushi rice recipe. The feel of sushi rice should be slightly sticky, perfect for shaping and holding ingredients.

Forming the Sushi

Creating nigiri is a trial and error process of pressing a small portion of sushi rice into a rectangular shape and topping it with the topping of your choice. For maki rolls, construction is a little more complicated. If you are planning to make sushi rolls, you should consider using a bamboo mat, as it makes rolling and pressing much easier.

First, lay your bamboo mat on the table or counter top with the flat side of the bamboo facing up and the string-tied edge facing away from you (so as not to tangle the strings in the sushi). Then place a sheet of nori on top, rough side up (nori has a smooth side and a rough side). This is important because you'll want your finished sushi roll to have the beautiful glossy side showing on the outside. Moisten your hands in a solution of water and vinegar and scoop up a palm-size portion of rice (about 1 cup). Place the rice in the center of the nori and spread with your fingers to a depth of approximately one quarter of an inch, stopping just short of both side edges and about an inch from the end sealing edge (edge with the bamboo mat string ties). At this point, some chefs spread a thin line of wasabi paste lengthwise across the roll in the center of the rice field.

Next, lay your filling ingredients lengthwise on top of the rice in the center. Do not over-stuff the rolls; this is a common "rookie mistake." When nori is pressed flat it looks like it is ready to have more added, yet all those extra ingredients will come out of the sides and top of the roll if you are not careful.

Next, lift up the edge of the mat closest to you with your thumbs and roll the nori over the ingredients into a cylinder, using the mat and your fingers to hold the fillings in place, tightening the roll firmly but gently as you go. Be careful not to press down too hard when rolling so as not to force the ingredients out of the sides. Remember that sushi rolls are not tortillas and should not be treated as such; they need to be treated gently. When you get to the sealing edge, place a few grains of rice in a row along the edge and press the nori layers together, using the rice grains like glue to seal the edge. Using both hands around the matted roll, tighten the roll, again firmly but gently. Unwrap the bamboo mat from the roll and tap/push in any rice at the ends that may be poking out (to compact the roll). Let it rest for a few minutes before slicing so that the nori becomes slightly moistened by the rice, making it less likely to crack.

Place the sushi seam-side down on a cutting board. Slightly dampen a very sharp knife with a vinegar-water solution (to prevent the rice from sticking) and slice using a firm downward stroke. Do not saw as this may cause the roll to fall apart. To get perfectly symmetrical slices, slice the roll in half first, then place the halves side by side and slice again into quarters, and again into eighths. Place the slices cut-side up and serve.

Sushi History: First referenced in manuals describing exotic foods served in tea houses, sushi was introduced to the United States in the 1890s. It was considered a delicacy and was served at the houses of the ultra sophisticated for cocktail hours and for other such functions. But sushi was not to become a mainstream Western entree for many years. Since then, Americans have explored many varieties of sushi and it has become quite popular almost everywhere in the world. Sushi preparation has evolved to include many ingredients such as exotic seafood and fish roe that would have been impossible without modern preservation technology.

Lesson 12
Sushi and Health

I keep my diet simple by sticking to mostly fruits and vegetables all day and then having whatever I want for dinner. I end up making healthy choices, like sushi or grilled fish, because I feel so good from eating well.
-Jennifer Morrison, Actress

If you are new to eating sushi one of the most important steps is to find a reputable sushi restaurant. If the fish is poorly prepared, it can turn you off from wanting to try sushi again. Check reviews online or go with friends who eat sushi often.

Some warning signs that the sushi quality may not be good are "all you can eat" for a fixed price, more than half of the available ingredients are cooked and menu items are not listed in Japanese.

If you are able to sit at the sushi bar you will be able to interact with the chef and also inspect the quality of the ingredients being used. Ask the chef or server for suggestions on what types of sushi and other items you should try when you are new to eating sushi.

Salmon, herring, mackerel, crab, and tuna are some of the fish and seafood used to make sushi and they are also high in omega-3 fatty acids which are associated with improving cholesterol levels and lowering blood pressure. These types of seafood and fish also contain other vitamins and minerals that are needed by your body.

It is possible to be exposed to bacteria, parasites, and viruses when eating uncooked fish, but this is rare, reputable chefs are able to serve raw fish in ways that are very safe. Different types of fish are prepared and preserved in different ways to make them safe for customers. Some fish, for example are frozen at a certain level to kill parasites. Some of the fish used in sushi such as tuna, marlin, shark, and swordfish can contain high levels of mercury, but as long as you are not eating these every day, most people will not have a problem from this. Consult your doctor if you have any questions about how sushi might affect you personally.

If you are trying to limit your grain consumption on a paleo/primal diet plan, remember white rice is the "least bad" of all the grains. White rice contains little or no of the "antinutrients," such as phytates and lectins, and contains no gluten.

Sushi History: Part of sushi's explosion in popularity in the United States in the 1980s was due to sushi being seen as a healthy alternative to the typical Western diet. Japanese people have lower rates of many health conditions, such as cancer and heart disease, than Americans.

Final Thoughts

*Just when you think you have a grasp on what
[sushi is] all about, you realize that
despite everything you think you've
learned, there's a whole lot more you
still don't know about the basics.*
-Dave Lowry, Author

Remember that when you eat sushi, you are getting a modern taste of a Japanese food tradition that has been around for hundreds of years. With the information in this book you will be able to walk into most any sushi restaurant in the world and have a great meal.

You have now finished reading all twelve lessons, but where should you go from here? This book is designed to be your first step in learning about sushi and becoming an expert. As your next step, we would like to welcome you to visit our resource guide and register for the additional information provided there. On our website we are able to provide information that is difficult to include in a book format, as mentioned throughout the text, plus we always offer free draft copies of our upcoming books to our subscribers.

To access the online guide, simply visit:
27Press.com/sushi

Final Tip: At this point, you may be wondering how you can retain all the information covered in this book. The best thing to do, of course, is get out there and try different types of sushi at different restaurants and figure out what you like. If you really want to memorize the important information covered in this book, check out one of the many "spaced-repetition" flashcard programs available on the internet and build a flashcard deck that covers the information you want to learn. Anki (available at ankisrs.net) is the best of these programs.

Online Resources

The text of this book is just the first step in what we provide to help you learn about sushi. Our online resource guide includes information that are not easy to convey in written formant, including everything mentioned throughout this book, plus the downloadable PDF companion: "12 Lessons On Sushi: The Complete Visual Guide."

Please visit **27Press.com/sushi** to register for our online resources.

About the Author/Publisher

27Press produces short, highly-informative guides on a variety of food and drink related topics. All our books are written and edited by professionals and reviewed by experts to produce the best possible guides.

We have upcoming books planned on chocolate, cigars, wine, coffee, Scotch, Bourbon, and more... Join our priority waitlist now for updates on future book releases:

27Press.com/waitlist

Check out our social media pages for more interesting information on these topics:

facebook.com/27Press

twitter.com/27Press

Feedback

Reviews on Amazon.com are the best way to give us feedback. Type the below address into your browser to be directed straight to Amazon's review page for this book. Then, simply click on the "Create your own review" button.

27press.com/amznsushi

You can also email us at any time with questions, comments, feedback, or suggestions.

news@27press.com

You can use the following pages to take
notes on your new sushi experiences.